MOLD, DOGS, AND SCIENTISTS

by David K. Soren

SCHOOL PUBLISHERS

Cover, ©Getty Images; p.3, ©Corbis; p.4, p.5, ©Larry Edwards/Zuma/Corbis; p.6, ©Stapleton Collection/Corbis; p.7, p.9, ©Peter Arnold, Inc./Alamy; p.8, ©Tony Freeman/Photo Edit; p.10, ©Woodfall Wild Images/Alamy; p.11, ©Bettmann/Corbis; p.12, ©J.G. Photography/Alamy; p.13, ©GmbH & Co. K.G./Alamy; p.14, (bl) ©Design Pics Inc./Alamy, (br) ©PCL/Alamy.

Copyright © by Harcourt, Inc.

All rights reserved. No part of this publication may be reproduced or transmitted in any form or by any means, electronic or mechanical, including photocopy, recording, or any information storage and retrieval system, without permission in writing from the publisher.

Requests for permission to make copies of any part of the work should be addressed to School Permissions and Copyrights, Harcourt, Inc., 6277 Sea Harbor Drive, Orlando, Florida 32887-6777. Fax: 407-345-2418.

HARCOURT and the Harcourt Logo are trademarks of Harcourt, Inc., registered in the United States of America and/or other jurisdictions.

Printed in China

ISBN 10: 0-15-351531-7
ISBN 13: 978-0-15-351531-6

Ordering Options
ISBN 10: 0-15-351214-8 (Grade 4 Advanced Collection)
ISBN 13: 978-0-15-351214-8 (Grade 4 Advanced Collection)
ISBN 10: 0-15-358121-2 (package of 5)
ISBN 13: 978-0-15-358121-2 (package of 5)

If you have received these materials as examination copies free of charge, Harcourt School Publishers retains title to the materials and they may not be resold. Resale of examination copies is strictly prohibited and is illegal.

Possession of this publication in print format does not entitle users to convert this publication, or any portion of it, into electronic format.

5 6 7 8 9 10 985 12 11 10 09

Have you ever seen a giraffe eating leaves and asked yourself, "Why is that giraffe's tongue so *purple*?" Have you ever watched a cat arch its back and wondered, "Why is it doing that?" Have you ever heard a dog bark and wondered, "What is it trying to say?" If you answered "yes" to any of these questions, then you probably think like a scientist.

Scientists have a lot of curiosity. They want to understand the world around them and what makes it work. As children, young scientists might ask questions like, "Why does it rain?" As adults, they wonder about things that humans still do not understand. Their questions may be more like, "Is there a black hole at the center of the universe?" or "Where have all my socks gone?"

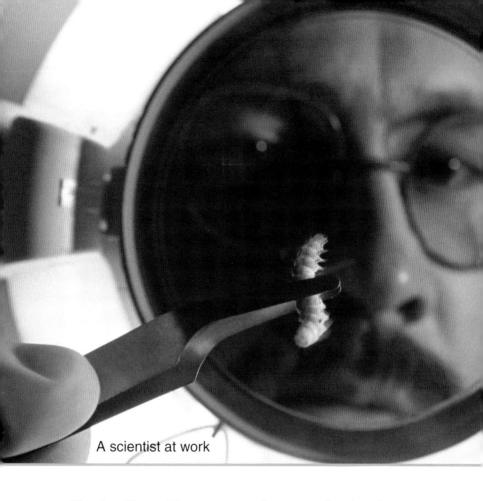
A scientist at work

Charles Henry Turner was a famous scientist. As
a child, he was constantly asking his parents questions.
Young Charles would sit outside, look at the world
around him, and wonder about the things he saw. Then
the questions would pour out of him. "Why are leaves
green? Where does wind come from? Why does the sky
look blue?"

4

Charles was so curious that he set out to find all the answers to his questions himself. He went to college and later became a teacher. All his life, though, he continued to study what fascinated him the most: insects.

Charles discovered a lot about insects. He was the first person to learn that insects can hear! The next time there's a fly on your arm, instead of swatting it, you can just say, "Fly, please go away now."

Charles also wondered how bees find their way back to their hive after flying around collecting honey all day. After all, there aren't any street signs or road maps for them to follow. Charles, being a dedicated scientist, made many observations of bees. He watched them closely and eventually found out that bees study the ground to find their way back. Maybe the flying bee says something like, "Okay, I take a right at the hill, a left at the strip of sand, and then head straight to my hive."

Charles also learned that bees can tell one color pattern from another. If a bee ever flies up to you, it might just be enjoying the pattern on your shirt!

Speaking of making observations, the scientist Edmund Halley once traveled all the way to a small island in the southern Atlantic Ocean just so he could look at the sky there! Halley was an English scientist who had many talents. He was very interested in astronomy—the study of outer space and the objects within it. He wanted to observe the stars in the Southern Hemisphere, so for eighteen months, on the island of St. Helena, Halley looked at the stars. In his quest to record what he had observed, he made the first map of the southern sky. He tinkered with the map until it eventually showed 341 stars!

Halley's Comet

    Halley returned to Europe, but, like a good astronomer, he kept his eyes on the sky. While traveling in France in 1682, he saw a bright comet passing across the night sky. A comet is a large ball of rock and ice that slowly orbits the sun. Comets have long "tails" of light that shine brightly.

    Halley and a friend continued to observe the comet. Now, do you think Halley just said, "My, what a pretty comet!"? No, he was too curious to leave it at that. Halley was also an excellent mathematician, so he did a little more research and found that comets had passed through the same part of the sky approximately every seventy-six years.

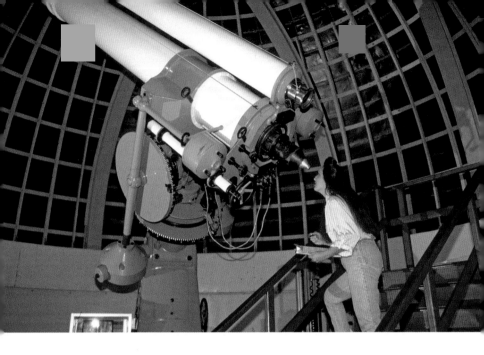

Based on the pattern he saw, Halley believed that each of those sightings was of the *same comet!* His idea was that this comet takes about seventy-six years to orbit the sun, so every seventy-six years or so, it passes by the Earth. Therefore, Halley figured out that the comet should appear again in the sky in December 1758.

Halley was not around to see whether or not he was correct. He died in 1742. However, on the night of December 25, 1758, a bright comet passed through the sky! Halley was absolutely right. Today, that comet is named *Halley's Comet,* after the great Edmund Halley. It is supposed to appear next in the year 2062. Be sure to mark your calendars!

You've seen it before—that strange green stuff growing on the sandwich you forgot about in the refrigerator. It's mold, and to most people, mold is disgusting and should be thrown away immediately. To Beatrix Potter, though, mold was fascinating.

Beatrix Potter was born in England in 1866. As a child, she enjoyed studying plants, animals, and insects. She would often draw or paint pictures of the things she studied. Nothing, though, was as interesting to her as fungi. Fungi are small living things like mold, mildew, and mushrooms.

Like any good scientist, Beatrix began to make detailed observations of different kinds of fungi. She also made beautiful drawings of fungi. By 1896, Beatrix had become a mycologist. A mycologist is an expert on fungi.

mold on strawberries

If you've ever had an aquarium, you've probably seen algae. That's the green stuff that grows all over the sides of the tank. Based on her observations, Beatrix developed a theory about algae. A theory is an idea a scientist has about something. Beatrix's theory was that algae joined with fungi to form something called lichen. Lichen are small living things that often grow on rocks and trees. You may have even trampled on some lichen while walking through the woods.

Beatrix wanted to discuss her findings about lichen with other scientists, but because she was a woman, they would only look at her drawings. Then she wrote a paper about her discovery and wanted to present it to fellow scientists. Again the other scientists would not allow it because she was a woman.

Beatrix was frustrated with these barriers. They made it hard for her to work with other scientists. She finally became discouraged and decided to give up being a scientist. She forged a new career for herself as an author.

Beatrix started writing and illustrating stories for children. Naturally, because of her interest in nature, the characters were animals. You may have even read some of her stories about Peter Rabbit and his family. Today, Beatrix Potter's Peter Rabbit books are still sold in stores! She became famous as an author even though her true love was science.

Years later, scientists stated that her theory about lichen was correct. The next time you read a Peter Rabbit story, remember that the person who wrote it was really a mold-loving scientist!

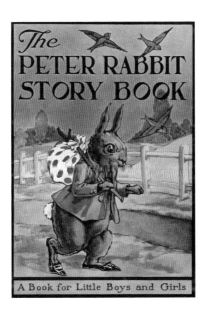

A delicious plate of food is placed in front of you. You are incredibly hungry, and it looks and smells so good. Your mouth starts to water. Why? That's something Russian scientist Ivan Pavlov wondered, too. Like other scientists, he decided to set up an experiment. Scientists set up experiments to test their theories. The results of an experiment can often tell the scientists whether their theories are correct or not.

People and animals salivate, or produce saliva, in their mouths. Saliva helps break down food so that it can be digested in the stomach. Pavlov had developed a theory he wanted to test. He believed that when people or animals salivated, a signal was sent to the stomach. The signal said, "Start digesting."

Pavlov wanted to see whether there were other ways to send that signal to the stomach, so he gathered up a few dogs for a special experiment. Did the dogs put on lab coats and hold Pavlov's test tubes? Probably not, but they did help him prove his theory.

Pavlov brought the dogs food. If you have ever known a dog, you know that, naturally, this made the dogs' mouths water. Of course, people do not salivate at the sight of dog food, but luckily for Pavlov, most dogs do. Anyway, Pavlov wanted to find out whether something other than food could send the signal to the stomach, so each time he gave the dogs the food, he rang a bell.

Guess what happened? After a while, all Pavlov had to do was ring the bell and the dogs' mouths would start watering! You see, the dogs had learned that the ringing bell meant that food was on the way. Pavlov had discovered something called the "law of conditioned reflex." To prove it was not a hoax, he studied this phenomenon for the next thirty years! Think about that: dog food and bells for thirty years!

Now you can see that scientists do a lot of observing. They come up with and perfect their theories. They set up experiments to test their theories. They also follow bees home, stare at the sky for months on end, draw pictures of mold, and make dogs drool for their dinner!

Think Critically

1. Is this book made up mostly of facts or opinions? Why do you think that is?

2. What did Charles Henry Turner learn about insects?

3. What did Pavlov's dogs do when he rang a bell?

4. How did Edmund Halley figure out that the comet named after him took about seventy-six years to orbit the sun?

5. What did you find surprising in this book? Why?

 ## Social Studies

Make a Time Line Pick out a scientist from this book or another scientist who interests you. Find out more about the scientist and what contributions the scientist made. Make a time line of the scientist's life and contributions to science.

School-Home Connection Discuss this book with a family member. Then talk about what you each think was the most important discovery or invention of all time.

Word Count: 1,504 (1,513)